P9-EDO-393

A Special Gift

FOR:

Mr Finiberg

FROM:

Jessica L.

DATE:

_8-25-97_

Dear Teacher™

Brownlow

Brownlow Publishing Company, Inc.

LITTLE TREASURES
MINIATURE BOOKS

Flowers for Graduation
For My Secret Pal
From Friend to Friend
Grandmothers are for Loving
Hope
Love
Mother—the Heart of the Home
My Sister, My Friend
Precious Are the Promises
Quilted Hearts
Rose Petals
Soft as the Voice of an Angel
The Night the Angels Sang
'Tis Christmas Once Again

Illustration Credits

CONTENTS

New Horizons

A teacher affects eternity;
no one can tell where his
influence stops.

— Henry Adams

Everyone is ignorant only
on different subjects.

—Will Rogers

Anytime you see a turtle up on top of a fence post, you know he had some help.

—Alex Haley

Cultivation of the mind is as necessary as food to the body.

— Cicero

The art of teaching is the art of assisting discovery.

MARK VAN DOREN

Education is what remains
when we have forgotten all
that we have been taught.

— Marquis of Halifax

What we do not call education
is more precious than which
we call so.

— Ralph Waldo Emerson

Three Things

There are three things to remember when teaching: know your stuff; know whom you are stuffing; and then stuff them elegantly.

— Lola May

Choose my instruction
instead of silver,
knowledge rather than
choice gold.

— Proverbs 8:10

Don't let failure go to
your head.

— Haim Ginott

The entire object of true
education is to make people
not merely to do the right
things, but to enjoy them;
not merely industrious, but
to love industry; not merely
learned, but to love knowledge; not merely pure, but
to love purity; not merely

just, but to hunger and
thirst after justice.

— John Ruskin

Everyone smiles in

the same language.

The end of learning is to repair the ruins of our first parents by regaining to know God aright, and out of that knowledge to love him, to imitate him, to be like him.

— John Milton

It's what we learn after we know it all that really counts.

— Anonymous

How Old Are You?

How old are you? Youth is not a time of life — it is a state of mind. You are as young as: your faith, your hope, your confidence. You are as old as: your doubt, your despair, your fear.

— H. B. Van Velzer

Do more than listen;
understand.
— John H. Rhoades

What we hope ever to do
with ease, we must learn
first to do with diligence.
— Samuel Johnson

A man should learn to sail
in all winds.

What the
teacher is, is
more important
than what he
teaches.

KARL MENNINGER

The true aim of everyone who aspires to be a teacher should be, not to impart his own opinion, but to kindle minds.

— Frederick W. Robertson

The object of education is to prepare the young to educate themselves throughout their lives.

— Robert Maynard Hutchins

The larger
the island of
knowledge, the
longer the shore line
of wonder.

RALPH W. SOCKMAN

Besides pride, loyalty, discipline, heart and mind, confidence is the key to all the locks.

— Joe Paterno

The object of teaching a child is to enable him to get along without his teacher.

— Elbert Hubbard

Before a man can wake
up and find himself
famous, he has to wake
up and find himself.

— Anonymous

The grandest homage
we can pay to truth is to
use it.

— Ralph Waldo Emerson

Long years must pass
before the truths we
have made for ourselves
become our very flesh.
— Vallery

The man who can make
hard things easy is the
educator.
— Ralph Waldo Emerson

Chapter Two

A Teacher's Heart

Teaching that impacts is not head to head, but heart to heart.

— Howard G. Hendricks

The happiest people don't necessarily have the best of everything. They just make the best of everything.

Uu Vv Ww Xx Yy Zz Aa Bb Cc

The Teacher's Psalm

The Lord is my teacher. I shall
not want. He maketh me to
learn in God's out-of-doors.
He teacheth me by his written
word. He instructeth my soul.
He guideth me in the paths of
true knowledge for his name's
sake. Yea, when the day's task
is done, and life's lessons have
been learned, I will fear no evil.
For thou wilt be with me, my

Teacher and my Comforter still.
Thou teachest even my enemies
to become pupils of the Great
Teacher. Thou leadest me
gently from the known to the
unknown. Thou givest me satis-
faction in my day's work. Surely
goodness and mercy shall follow
me all the days of my life, and I
shall be a learner in the school
of the Great Teacher forever.

— Frederic S. Goodrich

The one
thing worse
than a quitter
is the person
who is afraid
to begin.

I am not a teacher — only a fellow traveler of whom you asked the way. I pointed ahead — ahead of myself as well as of you.

— George Bernard Shaw

Give a little love to a child and you get a great deal back.

— John Ruskin

Every man who rises above
the common level has
received two educations:
the first from his teachers;
the second, more personal
and important, from himself.

— Edward Gibbon

Perhaps the most valuable result of all education is the ability to make yourself do the thing you have to do, when it ought to be done, whether you like it or not. This is the first lesson to be learned.

— Thomas Henry Huxley

A child miseducated
is a child lost.

JOHN F. KENNEDY

Children love to learn
but hate to be taught.

ANONYMOUS

Chapter Three

To Touch the Future

I touch the future. I teach.

— Christa McAuliffe

The only thing children wear out faster than shoes are parents and teachers.

— Anonymous

From the very beginning of his education, the child should experience the joy of discovery.

— Alfred North Whitehead

A young child, a fresh uncluttered mind, a world before him — to what treasures will you lead him?

— Gladys M. Hunt

He who helps a child helps humanity with an immediate-ness which no other help given to human creature in any other stage of human life can possibly give again.

— Phillips Brooks

The wildest colts make the best horses.

— Plutarch

Children have more need
of models than of critics.

— Joseph Foubert

Children will usually obey
if you explain patiently
what you want them to
do — and stand over
them while they do it.

May the Lord richly bless both you and your children.

—Psalm 115:14

The cost of educating a child today is immense. But the cost of not educating a child is incalculable.

Absolute Trust

All a child's life depends on the ideal it has of its parents. Destroy that and everything goes — morals, behavior, everything. Absolute trust in someone else is the essence of education.

— E. M. Forster

To make your children capable of honesty is the beginning of education.

Children are messengers we send to a time we will not see.

It is deviant behavior for an adolescent to be pleasant.

— Peggy Goldtrap

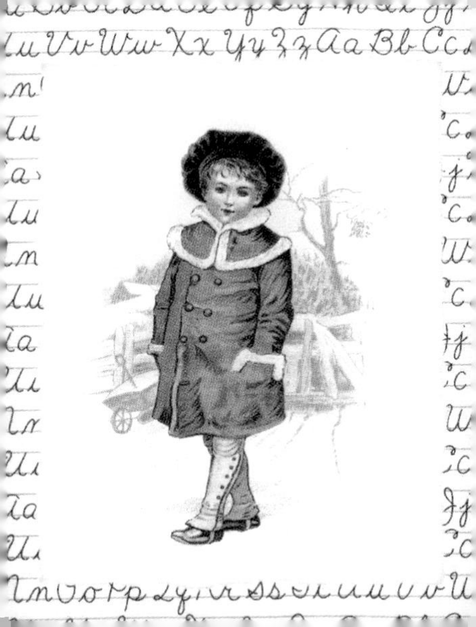
Vv Ww Xx Yy Zz Aa Bb

Men occasionally
stumble over the truth,
but most of them pick
themselves up and
hurry off as if nothing
happened.
— Winston Churchill

Where ignorance is bliss
'tis folly to be wise.

Few things help an individual more than to place responsibility upon him, and to let him know that you trust him.

— Booker T. Washington

It is wisdom to believe the heart.

Chapter Four

What is Wisdom?

Wisdom is more precious
than rubies.

— Proverbs 8:11

Let the wise listen and add
to their learning, and let the
discerning get guidance.

— Proverbs 1:5

Where can wisdom be found?
Where does understanding
  dwell?
Man does not comprehend
  its worth.
It cannot be bought with
  the finest gold,
Nor can its price be weighed
  in silver.
God understands the way to it
And he alone knows where
  it dwells.

— Job 28:12-23

This world belongs to the man who is wise enough to change his mind in the presence of facts.

— Roy L. Smith

The wise carry their knowledge as they do their watches — not for display, but for their own use.

The wise does at once
what the fool does at last.

— Baltasar Gracian

Dare to be wise; begin!
He who postpones the
hour of living rightly is like
the rustic who waits for
the river to run out before
he crosses.

— Horace

The invariable
mark of wisdom
is to see the
miraculous
in the common.

RALPH WALDO EMERSON

The art of
being wise is
the art of
knowing what
to overlook.

WILLIAM JAMES

The
cure for
boredom
is
curiosity.
There
is no
cure for
curiosity.

Chapter Five

Learning to Serve

The only ones among you
who will be really happy
are those who have sought
and found how to serve.

— Albert Schweitzer

Let love be your greatest
aim.

— 1 Corinthians 14:1

In praising or loving a child,
we love and praise not that
which is, but that which we
hope for.

— Goethe

Belief is truth held in the
mind; faith is a fire in the
heart.

— Joseph Fort Newton

If you want to become
the greatest in your
field, no matter what it
may be, equip yourself
to render greater service
than anyone else.

— Clinton Davidson

The pursuit of the truth
shall set you free — even if
you never catch up with it.

Wisdom is oft times
nearer when we stoop
than when we soar.

— William Wordsworth

I have chosen the way of
truth;
I have set my heart on
your laws.
I hold fast to Your statutes,
O Lord;
do not let me be put to
shame.
I run in the paths of Your
commands,
for You have set my heart
free.

— Psalm 119:30-32

I find that a great part of
the information I have was
acquired by looking up
something else on the way.
— Franklin P. Adams

It wasn't until quite late in life
that I discovered how easy it
is to say, "I don't know."
— W. Somerset Maugham

If I can put one thought of rosy sunset into the life of any man or woman, I shall feel that I have worked with God.

— George MacDonald

Our greatest glory consists not in never falling, but in rising every time we fall.

— Oliver Goldsmith

Learning makes the wise wiser and the fool more foolish.

— John Ray

The best way for a student to get out of difficulty is to go through it.

What we have to learn to do, we learn by doing.

— Aristotle

Great works are performed
not by strength but by
perseverance.

— Samuel Johnson

The educator should be
the "leading learner."

— Thomas Groome

The secret of education
lies in respecting the pupil.

— Ralph Waldo Emerson

Chapter Six

Light a Candle

We must view young
people not as empty
bottles to be filled, but
as candles to be lit.

— Robert H. Shaffer

There are no bad students,
only discouraged ones.

School is a building that has four walls — with tomorrow inside.

— Lon Watters

One cool judgment is worth a thousand hasty councils. The thing to do is to supply light and not heat.

— Woodrow Wilson

I have four things to learn
   in life:
To think clearly without
      hurry or confusion;
To love everybody sincerely;
To act in everything with
      the highest motives;
To trust in God
      unhesitatingly.
      — Helen Keller

We leave traces of our-
selves wherever we go,
on whatever we touch.

— Lewis Thomas

I don't know the key to
success, but the key to
failure is trying to please
everybody.

— Bill Cosby

Use what talents you have
— the woods would be
silent if no bird sang except
those that sing best.

Man's mind stretched to a
new idea never goes back
to its original dimensions.

— Oliver Wendell Holmes

It is better to learn late—
than never.

Influence

James A. Garfield said that
a log with a student on one
end and Mark Hopkins, his
old teacher, on the other
end was his ideal college.
The point in it all is that
personal contact and direct
interest in the individual

student by an instructor
of lofty character is the
main thing in any institution
of learning.

— F. S. Groner

The roots of education are bitter, but the fruit is sweet.

— Aristotle

I am not a teacher, but an awakener.

— Robert Frost

The fear of the Lord is the beginning of wisdom.

—Psalm 111:10

Only when
the heart
loves can the
intellect
do great work.

N. D. HILLIS

It is easier
to move a cemetery
than to effect
a change in
curriculum.

WOODROW WILSON

Zebra
Zeal
Zephyr
Zouave

Z is the letter that's last to appear,
So this is the end of the book, my dear.